D1295493

REVIEW COPY
COURTESY OF
CAPSTONE PRESS

Vert Skating:
Mastering the Ramp

by Jeff Savage

Capstone
press

Mankato, Minnesota

Edge Books are published by Capstone Press
151 Good Counsel Drive, P.O. Box 669, Mankato, Minnesota 56002
www.capstonepress.com

Library of Congress Cataloging-in-Publication Data
Savage, Jeff.
    Vert skating: mastering the ramp / by Jeff Savage.
    p. cm.—(Edge books. Skateboarding)
    Includes bibliographical references and index.
    ISBN 0-7368-2705-6 (hardcover)
    1. Skateboarding—Juvenile literature. I. Title.
GV859.8.S29 2005
796.22—dc22   2004000664

Summary: Describes vert skating, a sport in which skateboarders do tricks on halfpipe ramps.

Editorial Credits
James Anderson, editor; Timothy Halldin, series designer; Enoch Peterson, book designer; Jo Miller, photo researcher; Eric Kudalis, product planning editor

Photo Credits
AP/Wide World Photos/Tony Dejak, 15
Capstone Press/Gary Sundermeyer, 10–11
Corbis/NewSport/Al Fuchs, 12; Larry Kasperek, 16
Getty Images, 28; Ezra Shaw, 4, 21, 26; Stanley Chou, 8
Mercury Press/Isaac Hernandez, 22
Mira/Carl Schneider, 7
Patrick Batchelder, 24
SportsChrome Inc./Michael Zito, cover
Unicorn Stock Photos/Aneal N. Vohra, 19

Edge Books thanks Tod Swank, member, Board of Directors, International Association of Skateboard Companies, for his assistance in preparing this book.

1 2 3 4 5 6 09 08 07 06 05 04

Table of Contents

Bob Burnquist did a 540 at the 2001 X Games.

What Is Vert?

Bob Burnquist stands on his skateboard and drops in on the ramp. He glides across the ramp and gains speed. Burnquist is at the 2001 X Games in Philadelphia. Nearly 20,000 fans have filled the First Union Center to see pro skaters do great moves.

Burnquist shoots up the ramp and into the air. He spins and flips at the same time. He does a somersault as he spins one and one-half times before landing. He has done a perfect 540. He coasts across to the other side. He goes up the ramp and gets big air. He flips the board with his feet. He lands backward to complete a kick flip to fakie.

Learn About

- ⬭ **Bob Burnquist**
- ⬭ **Vert beginnings**
- ⬭ **Halfpipes**

Burnquist lands more tricks during his run. Every move is perfect. The judges give him the highest scores, and he wins the gold medal. Skateboarding superstar Tony Hawk calls Burnquist's run the best he has ever seen.

All About Vert

Vert is a popular skateboarding style. Vert skating is done on vert ramps or in empty concrete pools. The word vert is short for vertical. It means up and down. The walls of a vert ramp are vertical.

Vert skating started in the 1960s. Skaters in California practiced in empty swimming pools. They rode their boards up the sides and back down. By the 1970s, skaters had built ramps to take the place of pools.

Halfpipes

Skaters call vert ramps halfpipes because they are shaped like half of a pipe. They are U-shaped. Today's halfpipes are usually between 8 and 12 feet (2.4 and 3.7 meters) high.

A vert skater does moves on a halfpipe ramp.

Halfpipes are usually made of wood and steel. A steel edge runs across the top of the ramp. This edge is called the coping. Some skaters grind and slide their boards across the coping. Skaters also grab the coping to do handplants.

The areas where the vertical walls curve to the flat bottom are called transitions. Skaters gain speed as they cross the transitions.

With enough speed, skaters get air. They do tricks above the coping. Vert skaters spin, twist, turn, and grab before dropping back in on the ramp.

Skaters do moves above a ramp's coping.

Halfpipe Diagram

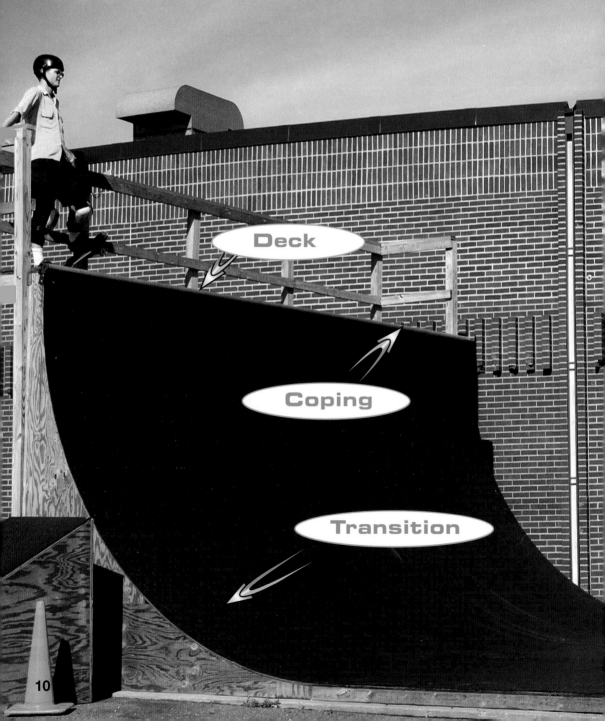

Deck

Coping

Transition

Transition

Flat

Skaters balance on the ramp's deck when they drop in.

Basic Moves

Vert skaters have different styles. Some skate fast and get big air. Others stay close to the ramp. They do grinds and slides on the coping. But all skaters share some common basic moves.

Dropping In

To enter a halfpipe, skaters stand on the deck and drop in. Dropping in is vert skating's most basic move. Skaters stand with their back foot on the back edge of the board. The back of the board is on the coping. The front of the board hangs over the edge. The skaters lean forward and bend their knees. They glide down into the ramp.

Learn About

- Entering a halfpipe
- Kick turns
- Frontside and backside

13

Getting Air

In 1979, Alan Gelfand learned how to get air without even grabbing his board. He stepped down on the tail of his board. He slid his front foot forward. The front of his board rose in the air. He then tucked his back foot toward his body. The skateboard stayed on his feet. People called this trick the ollie. "Ollie" is Gelfand's nickname. The ollie is part of most skating moves.

Skaters get air any time they rise above the coping. To get air, some skaters do an ollie. The move allows skaters to lift their boards above the coping.

Skaters do a move that is like a backward ollie called a nollie. When skaters do nollies, the backs of their boards rise in the air.

Turns

During most vert moves, skaters shoot into the air and turn before landing. Turning the direction that their toes point is called a frontside. Turning toward their heels is called a backside.

Skaters turn toward their toes during a frontside.

When skaters turn and land backward, they do a fakie. Any move can be done fakie when the skater lands backward.

Skaters sometimes turn their bodies after they have landed. Skaters land in one direction then do a half turn during a revert. They then go down the ramp in the opposite direction.

Skaters try for big spins at competitions.

CHAPTER THREE

Advanced Moves

Skaters start out with basic moves. Some skaters move on to harder moves. They do spins, grinds, and combos. A few of these skaters even become pros. They do their moves at contests such as the Gravity Games and the X Games.

Spins and Inverts

Spins are a big part of vert tricks. Skaters talk about spins like circles. A full circle is 360 degrees. Skaters call a full spin a 360. They call a half spin a 180. One and one-half spins is called a 540. Two and one-half spins is a 900. Tony Hawk was the first skater to land the 900 in competition.

Learn About

- Tony Hawk
- McTwist
- Stalefish

17

The invert is a popular advanced move. Skaters go above the ramp with their feet in the air. They grab the coping and hold the board to their feet. After a short pause, they drop back into the ramp backward. Bobby Valdez created this trick. Eddie Elguera changed it by dropping in frontside.

Grinds and Slides

Skaters do grinds and slides along the coping. They grind on the trucks of their boards. Trucks are the metal parts that connect the wheels to the board. A 50-50 is a grind on both trucks. A nose grind is a grind on only the front truck. To do a Smith grind, skaters grind on the back truck and the side of the board.

Skaters slide on the underside of their boards. To do a nose slide, skaters slide on the board's nose. During a tail slide, skaters slide on the back of the board.

A skater grabs the coping during an invert.

Blunt

A blunt is another move skaters do on the coping. In this move, skaters let two wheels and a truck rest against the ramp's deck. The tail or nose is flat against the wall of the ramp. Skaters then do a small ollie to pop back into the ramp. They land on their wheels.

Skaters have changed blunts in many ways. Some skaters do nose blunts, blunt slides, and blunt 180s frontside and backside.

Combos

Vert skaters often combine two tricks to create new tricks. Skaters call these moves combos. An example is the kick flip Indy. Skaters do a kick flip, then grab the toe side of the board with their back hand. They pin the board to their feet.

Skaters have no limits to the number of combo moves they create. Skaters might do a backside Smith grind with a revert. Another combo move is a frontside ollie nose blunt.

Pro skaters combine tricks to make difficult moves.

Signature Moves

Sometimes when skaters invent tricks, other skaters name the trick after the trick's inventor. These tricks are signature moves. Mike McGill created the McTwist in 1985. McGill combined a 540 with a frontside flip.

Some tricks are named by accident. Tony Hawk invented the stalefish. The move is an ollie combined with a backside grab. After doing the move, Hawk described some fish he was eating from a can as stale fish. Another skater thought Hawk was naming his new move. The name stuck.

Tony Hawk did a 900 at the 2003 X Games.

The 900

When skaters compete at events, fans expect them to do their signature moves. If the move is spectacular, the fans cheer for it even more.

In 1999, Tony Hawk did a 900 at the X Games. Fans were shocked as Hawk spun two and one-half times in midair. But Hawk's amazing move came too late in his run. His time was up and the move didn't count.

Hawk continued to practice the 900. In 2003, he finally landed the move during a timed run. At the Summer X Games, he won gold in the vert skating best trick event. Fans often ask Hawk to do the 900 when he skates.

Halfpipes are popular in many small skateparks.

Ramps and Events

Vert skaters in most areas can find skateparks that have vert ramps. They are not all in big cities. Dry Run Creek Park in Mitchell, South Dakota, has a halfpipe 5 feet (1.5 meters) high. Bennington Skatepark in Bennington, Vermont, has an 8-foot (2.4-meter) vert ramp. Plunkett Park in Mexico, Missouri, has a halfpipe that is 5.5 feet (1.7 meters) high.

Learn About

- Great skateparks
- X Games
- Vans Triple Crown

Danny Way skated in two events at the 2001 X Games.

Trivia In 1997, Danny Way set the record for getting the biggest air. He soared 16.5 feet (5 meters) above the coping. Way broke his own record in 2002. He reached 18 feet, 3 inches (5.5 meters) above the coping.

Pro Vert Ramps

Vert ramps for pro events can be 12 feet (3.7 meters) high or more. The largest ramp ever built stood 18 feet (5.5 meters) tall.

Halfpipes are often built just for pro events. These ramps include the halfpipe in Panama Beach, Florida, and the ramp in Asbury Park, New Jersey. The halfpipe at the Oceanside Pier and Amphitheater in Oceanside, California, was also built for pro events.

Big Competitions

Pro vert events have become very popular. Several companies sponsor events worldwide. Thousands of fans come to see the top vert skaters. Some of these events are also shown on TV around the world.

In 1995, the ESPN TV network held an event called the Extreme Games. In the second year, ESPN changed the name to the X Games. Vert skating takes place each year at the Summer X Games.

The X Games aren't the only popular vert skating competition. ESPN sponsors other X Games events around the world. Skaters take part in the Asian X Games and the Latin American X Games. Another event is the Vans Triple Crown of Skateboarding. This event has the world's best skaters competing for prize money.

Other events include the Gravity Games, Mountain Dew National Championships, Vans Slam City Jam, and the Xbox World Championship. Thousands of fans watch as pro skaters show off their signature moves at these events.

Vert skating becomes more popular each year. Young skaters watch pro events like the X Games on TV. They practice the moves at local skateparks. As the young skaters get better, they invent new moves. These young skaters make sure that vert skating will continue to be popular.

Skaters around the world take part in vert events.

Glossary

coping (KO-ping)—the metal bar at the top of a halfpipe

handplant (HAND-plant)—a handstand on the edge of a halfpipe

signature (SIG-nuh-chur)—a move or a way to do a move; skaters become known for signature moves.

somersault (SUHM-ur-sawlt)—a trick in which a skater flips in a complete circle forward or backward

sponsor (SPON-sur)—when a company pays the cost of hosting an event in exchange for advertising its name and product

transition (tran-ZISH-uhn)—the curved areas of a halfpipe between the vertical walls and the flat bottom

Read More

Braun, Eric. *Tony Hawk*. Amazing Athletes. Minneapolis: Lerner, 2004.

Doeden, Matt. *Skateparks: Grab Your Skateboard.* Skateboarding. Mankato, Minn.: Capstone Press, 2002.

Stout, Glenn. *On the Halfpipe with Tony Hawk*. Boston: Little Brown and Company, 2001.

Internet Sites

FactHound offers a safe, fun way to find Internet sites related to this book. All of the sites on FactHound have been researched by our staff.

Here's how:

1. Visit *www.facthound.com*
2. Type in this special code **0736827056** for age-appropriate sites. Or enter a search word related to this book for a more general search.
3. Click on the **Fetch It** button.

FactHound will fetch the best sites for you!

Index